WHAT IS STEAM?

THE SCIENCE IN STEAM

BY THERESA EMMINIZER

Please visit our website, www.garethstevens.com. For a free color catalog of all our high-quality books, call toll free 1-800-542-2595 or fax 1-877-542-2596.

Cataloging-in-Publication Data
Names: Emminizer, Theresa.
Title: The science in STEAM / Theresa Emminizer.
Description: New York : Gareth Stevens Publishing, 2024. | Series: What is STEAM? | Includes glossary and index.
Identifiers: ISBN 9781538285534 (pbk.) | ISBN 9781538285541 (library bound) | ISBN 9781538285558 (ebook)
Subjects: LCSH: Science–Juvenile literature.
Classification: LCC Q163.E46 2023 | DDC 503–dc2

Published in 2024 by
Gareth Stevens Publishing
2544 Clinton Street
Buffalo, NY 14224

Designer: Leslie Taylor
Editor: Theresa Emminizer

Photo credits: Series Art (background art) N.Savranska/Shutterstock.com; Cover chomplearn/Shutterstock.com; p. 5 wavebreakmedia/Shutterstock.com; p. 7 zlikovec/Shutterstock.com; p. 9 David Pereiras/Shutterstock.com; p. 11 NIKS ADS/Shutterstock.com; p. 13 Anastassiya Bezhekeneva/Shutterstock.com; p. 15 A3pfamily/Shutterstock.com; p. 17 Kat Om/Shutterstock.com; p. 19 Dejan Dundjerski/Shutterstock.com; p. 21 Ilike/Shutterstock.com.

Printed in the United States of America

CPSIA compliance information: Batch #CSGS24: For further information contact Gareth Stevens at 1-800-542-2595.

CONTENTS

Boldface words appear in the glossary.

What STEAM Stands For

STEAM is short for science, technology, **engineering**, art, and math. These subjects are very different in some ways. But they're all about **exploring** how things work. In this book, you'll learn about the science in STEAM.

What Is Science?

Science is a way of studying and understanding the world around us. Scientists make **observations**. They ask questions about why things happen the way they do. They look for answers by coming up with ideas and testing them to see if they're true.

The Scientific Method

The scientific method is a set of steps used by scientists. The first step is to gather information, or facts. The next is to form a hypothesis, or guess based on what they know. They then test the hypothesis with an **experiment**.

Scientists record, or write down, the **results** of their experiment. They analyze the results. To analyze something is to think deeply about what it might mean. Lastly, scientists form a conclusion, or judgment about what they've learned.

Earth and Space Science

There are many ways to study the world around us. That's why there are many different branches, or kinds, of science! Earth science is all about our planet, or world. Space science is the study of outer space, the stars, and other planets.

Life Science

Life science is all about life and living things, such as animals, bugs, and plants. It also has to do with life processes, such as how a creature eats, sleeps, grows, or has babies. Life science is sometimes called biology.

Physical Science

Physical science has to do with nonliving things. Chemistry is the study of chemicals, or matter which can be mixed with other matter to cause changes. Physics is the study of matter and the forces that act on it.

Science Skills

No matter what branch they study, all scientists share a set of skills. Scientists must be curious, or interested in the world. They must look closely at the things around them. They must ask questions. They must think outside the box to look for answers.

Are You a Scientist?

Are you curious about the world you live in? Do you love learning about animals or plants? Are you **fascinated** by outer space? Do you find yourself asking questions and trying out experiments? Science might be the path for you!

GLOSSARY

engineering: The use of science and math to build better objects, or things.

experiment: A scientific test in which you carry out a series of actions and watch what happens in order to learn about something.

explore: To search in order to find out new things.

fascinated: Strongly interested in or excited about something.

observation: To make note of something after watching carefully.

result: Something that comes about as an effect or an end.

FOR MORE INFORMATION

BOOKS

Brundle, Joanna. *Classroom to Career: My Job in Science.* New York, NY: PowerKids Press 2021.

Nelson, Louise. *Magnetic Slime.* New York, NY: Windmill Books, 2022.

WEBSITES

Kids Environment Kids Health
kids.niehs.nih.gov/activities/science-experiments/index.htm
Try out fun science experiments!

NASA Science
spaceplace.nasa.gov/science/en/
Learn how to think scientifically by asking questions and making observations.

INDEX